GRAMMAR TEACHING

GRAMMAR TEACHING

A Waldorf Approach to the Teaching of the Grammar of the Mother Tongue in the Lower School

BRIEN MASTERS

Wynstones Press

Published by:

Wynstones Press

Stourbridge

England

www.wynstonespress.com

First published in 2012 by Perevale Publications

Second edition Wynstones Press 2019

Layout: Ian Botting and Wynstones Press

Front cover design: Brien Masters

Printed in UK.

ISBN 9780 946206 834

Contents

An Acknowledgement

from the first edition

Dear Colleague,

The verse of Rudolf Steiner's which begins 'We have the will to work', often spoken first thing in the school day, as part of the living spiritual foundation on which the educational life of a school is built, is a rare occurrence in that it is couched in the first person plural. This fact resonated strongly in me again a few weeks ago, when a colleague at Michael Hall in England, suggested that the present work be written on grammar teaching of the mother tongue in the Lower School.

It is not a topic that most class teachers would place closest to their heart – for one teacher that pride of place will be held by, say, mechanics or astronomy in Class 7; for another it will be Norse mythology in Class 4 and so on. In fact, in the general educational climate that has prevailed over the last decades – not exactly a phenomenon of cultural global warming – many are either hazy about the grammar of their mother tongue, hearing of its importance in Waldorf education during their initial teacher training with a considerable degree of surprise and even alarm, or finding the pedagogical skill required to teach the subject, once they stand in the classroom, more of a stone to be rolled away than a descending Whitsuntide tongue of fire. Nevertheless, handicaps are there to be uncapped, obstacles to be overcome and difficulties to be turned to good account. Realising what awakening to grammar can do for the child's development of character can became a sun which dispels the haze of insufficient rationale, or an inner force which rolls away the stone of inadequate methodology.

If the jottings in the present slim volume assist in whichever of these processes colleagues may find themselves, it will have served its purpose – a purpose, now I come to think of it, unstated by the Michael Hall colleague who first raised the matter. The enthusiasm in his voice of 'we have the will to work, that into this our work *may flow*' etc. was enough in itself of a prompt.

It is therefore with appreciation and gratitude to Nino Radojcin the question-popper, to his colleagues in the Lower School who expressed their corporate support for the project, to Liz Attwell and Josie Alwyn, experienced Upper School English specialists, who likewise were eager to support something which would help give a strong foundation for what the adolescent needs from the English lesson, to Chris Marshall and the School management team who warmly endorsed the proposal that Michael Hall be the distributor for the first edition of the volume, and to Ian Botting whose fine sense of reader-friendliness affected the clear layout of the book, which he also personally effected in order to make its contents as accessible as possible to busy teachers. So it is with thankful acknowledgements to these colleagues, all of them beavering away under the star-blessed roof of Michael Hall Rudolf Steiner School, that I sign off with the hope that their express goodwill will bear fruit in the lives of teachers and children alike, far and near.

Brien Masters
Palm Sunday 2012
Sussex, England

Why Grammar?

Very broadly speaking, in the twentieth century approach to the teaching of grammar, the pendulum swung in opposite directions, from sheer neglect or deliberate ostracising to a pounding-hammer insistence on the subject which was rooted in the fact that the Classics necessitated a thorough acquaintance with grammatical constructions (endings of parts of speech – its nouns and verbs with their accompanying adverbs and adjectives), in order to extract the exact meaning of what the ancient authors had to say. Rudolf Steiner appeared to have no quarrel with the latter, but gave the teaching of the mother tongue a position in the child's experience which was a lighthouse in educational psychology, whose beams announced the whereabouts of a harbour for the ego hitherto unrealised. In short, its teaching *strengthened the ego.* But how? And how are we to understand this?

Of the four basic members of our constitution, physical, etheric, astral and ego, the ego is something of a revolutionary, not abiding by the septennial rhythm of the other members, the sheaths into which it incarnates. It delights in Loki-ing its way into the business of life. Our first three human achievements – to stand upright and freely *walk*, to *speak* the language into which we are 'born', and to *make sense* of the galaxy of percepts that our sponge-like sense-life soaks up through thinking – are like responses taking place on the physical plane at the behest of the ego which still remains in the lap of the gods. It is as if the legs of the new-born baby thrill at the thought of responding to the call from on high: "Engage with the earth and exult in lifting against its gravitational pull;" as if the heart and soul resonate to the discovering of other hearts and souls: "Connect with your fellow humans through the gift of speech;" as if the mind fills with the twinkling light of a myriad stars, pin-pricking through the canopy of the heavens: "Attend to your inner life wherein can be found the Jacob's ladder to your other home;" all of which fountains forth as ego-triumph, like water struck from a rock in the Sinai, when the c.3-year-old says "I".

Now in all this, despite the highly individual variation that each toddler may 'perform' on the theme, there is the self-evident *sequence* of walking, talking, thinking and saying "I". Perhaps there exist remote exceptions to the order of the sequence that have not yet come my way. However, for the present purposes, it will be useful to think of the sequence not as three-fold – the first three achievements of the child, the hallmark of its humanity – but as four-fold. The mountain of life appears at birth – first the valley of *walking* below, second the lower slopes of *speaking* as we head away from the valley, third the steep ascent of *thinking* culminating in its peak – and finally the dawn of the ego as the mountain is flooded with the light of sunrise. This merely serves to emphasise that most, if not all of those first three achievements, precede whatever incision of consciousness is represented by *the saying of "I", unbidden by the outer world.*

To add to this: it is a commonplace that we have comparatively few, if any, memories of those early years, family photograph albums notwithstanding. Similarly with other situations in life when the ego is not present within its sheaths. Foremost among examples of this are the oblivion of deep sleep, and the billion and one sense perceptions that impinge upon us every day of life to which the attention of the ego is not turned sufficiently for them to register. Memory is not a cine camera spool of every thought and sense perception (thank goodness): memory is a store of that on which the ego has zoom-lensed its conscious attention, sometimes zooming closely, at other times more distantly. And for present purposes we can leave aside the familiar problem of not being able to find where, amongst the towering stack which memory stores, is the place we need at a given moment. Suffice it to say that we have acquired the uprightness of standing and walking, the acquisition of speech and the intricacies of thinking *before* the peak of the mountain enjoys the floodlit world of its ego dawn. Hence, *learning* to speak does not reside in the memory.

Speaking, moreover, includes the wealth of *vocabulary* that embodies the experience of both the outer and inner worlds in which we live, the *music of the language* (the sing-song vowels of a game-keeper in the Grampian Highlands, the guttural mystery of certain Arabic vowels, the consonantal goulash of Slav languages that adds percussive gush to its melody, for instance), the thought forms which manifest in languages as different *syntax* and – what we are mainly concerned with here – that which is universal in principle: the mystery of *grammar*. In speaking we have the remarkable phenomenon that, before the child has said "I", and before the accumulative acquisition of memories which follow, he or she is skiing down the slopes of grammar while coming a cropper less and less _ and that refers only to external croppers. Furthermore, even when the two-year-old points to the rice pudding and says, "More," there is contained in that single word the grammatical implication of, "Please can I have another helping of that deliciously warm, creamy-smooth, soft-on-the-tongue-and-gums, sweet-on-the-taste-buds, infusing-my-well-being-with-happiness, white stuff in that pyrex dish." This is tantamount to saying that the child virtually speaks in *interjections*, so that the "more" is no more and no less than the grammatical panorama of 'Jack', as he huddles invisibly – interjection-like – condensed, tense and crumpled beneath the lid of his Jack-in-the-box, waiting for the catch holding the lid down to be flicked open, so that he can leap and spring jubilantly into the rhetorical air of articulate speech.

From this beginning, the river of each language's grammatical construction wends and winds through the landscape of life until Class 3 where, being Jack-in-the-boxed into the first glimmerings of grammar awareness, it strengthens the ego – as the following pages will seek to elucidate!

Notes

Notes

Class 3

Noun, Verb, Adjective

Frequently when Rudolf Steiner referred to the Loki-like incision of the ego into the second septennial phase of childhood, he did so by using the term the 9th/10th year. This would suggest that the incision, though slow and most certainly incisive – the other term of reference, the *Rubicon*, is sufficient to indicate its no-going-back incisiveness – and though at times a crossroads – like shock to the system, can spread itself over as much as two years. Translated into the Waldorf Lower School, this means Classes 3 and 4. It is essentially into the first of these, Class 3, that is when the child is turning nine years of age, that the consciousness of grammar, as indicated above, is raised, the first focus being on the *parts of speech*.

The two schools of thought – either to start by immediately giving an overview of all nine parts of speech, or to concentrate on a smaller number as a first step, and then work through the others, class by class – can both be justified. However, as the subject provides such a vital prop to the ego when it descends into the vale of the Rubicon and experiences thereby the dwindling support of the spiritual ground on which it had relied during its early years of childhood, it is essential that the prop be thoroughly adequate. One needs to bear in mind, therefore, that the consciousness of an 8/9-year-old is not one in which the benefit to the ego of raising from its deep well the awareness of the grammatical 'know-how' that was achieved with the acquisition of speech prior to the "I" milestone passed during the first three years, can be effected by hauling on a rope of intellect. The success of the raising requires a largely participative methodology. This will ensure that the stage of child development which has been reached in these years has amplest room for play. And, as we shall see, most of the parts of speech can be shown to have an inner rapport with later stages of development, right up to and including Class 7. This does not preclude pursuing the overview approach (the first school of thought), but it does favour (a) concentrating on a small number of parts of speech as a getting-off-to-a-good-start in Class 3; followed by (b) a revision of what has gone before in succeeding years; and (c) an additional focus on those 'parts' which chime particularly harmoniously with the age and stage of the child's changing consciousness in Classes 4, 5 and 6. As this is manifestly symbiotic with the Waldorf maxim of teaching those subjects (both the 'what' and the 'how') which are best suited to midwifing the stage of development which the child is traversing each year, it is the approach to grammar teaching that will be followed here.

Nevertheless, it is worth having a route card of the full journey before setting out: i.e. verb, noun and adjective (Class 3); adverb, pronoun and preposition (Class 4); conjunction (Class 5); article (Class 6), and interjection (Class 7).

Notes

Notes

The three-foldness of verb, noun and adjective is particularly helpful in Class 3 at the outset of the journey. With them (indeed, with only noun and verb) complete sentences can be formed:

{God created mountains.}
{Tilers climb ladders.}
{Cows moo. Donkeys bray. Hens cluck. Pigs grunt.}
and perhaps
{Come! Help Mummy.}.

In order to lift the subject as much as possible out of its potentially intellectual dryness – the main off-putting danger of grammar teaching – most teachers invent nomenclature that concurs with the young child's participative consciousness. Verbs tell you what is being done: they are *doing words* or *action words*:

{harvesting, hammering, wandering, thinking, parting [the Red Sea], deciding, decided, swam}.

Nouns tell you what something is called: they are (some)*thing words* or *name words*:

{cheese, Somerset, bell-ringing, Paradise, oats, spirit-level, Melchior, difficulties, archangel, growth, ballast, sap, yeast, heat, government, College of Teachers}.

Adjectives describe, characterise or portray what things are like, how they appear or sound or smell: they are *how words*, or *describing words*:

Notes

{green, tall, wooden, smelly, soft, delicious, terrifying, comfortable, useful}.

We may wish to take the step in class that reveals the soul's threefold connection with its bodily seat. We feel if something is nice or nasty, friendly or threatening, pleasant or ugly; describing words relate to our *feeling-ful heart*. Doing words involve *limbs* if they refer to outer action , but we also sense the inner action of:

{choosing, guessing, pretending}.

Name words sit invisibly, like a cap on the head of things. In this grouping the anthropocentric nature of Waldorf education is expressed. And perhaps we encourage the children to colour-code the parts of speech – at least at this early stage:

{Young (green) children (blue) play (red).}.
{Wise farmers grow healthy, nutritious wheat.}
{Cows give excellent manure.}
{Kings' palaces can be magnificent.}
{Dying swans are known to sing.}
{Architects design buildings.}
and perhaps
{Rocking chairs are fun.}.

Notes

From the outset it can be of benefit if the children are *inventive* participators in the examples that the lesson furnishes and invites. For instance, one grammar 'game' the children may enjoy would be choosing a place (such as *beach* in the following example) and making up rhymes – the underlined parts of the rhyme are given them as a template:

On the *beach* are thing words, basking in the sun:
parasol, donkey, sand-castle, fun.

Doing words a-plenty are found there too:
splashing, sailing, paddling, whaling, run, jump, do.

On the following day, they can move from the beach to the Garden of Paradise, or to the farm, or (if there still is one nearby) to the High Street. Once the sentence is richly and sturdily accoutred with the visor, breastplate and lance of grammar, it may confidently ride forth to conquer the rest of the field.

Class 4

Adverb, Preposition, Pronoun

Following on from the previous chapter, the question arises: Would not *adverbs* qualify for inclusion in Class 3 grammar alongside adjectives? Just as the adjective brings a feeling element towards the noun, so does the *adverb* bring a qualifying element, reflected in feeling, to the verb. Why wait, therefore, till Class 4 to introduce adverbs when the threefoldness of the noun and verb polarity, with the adjective lying between, is already in place? Philosophically, the argument appears strengthened by the fact that '*the middle*' can often be identified by its twofold nature – typically and archetypally, of course, heart and lung; and equally archetypal though less obvious at first sight by looking at rhythm (the 'beat' of heart and lung' with their average 72 : 18 per minute ratio) from the perspective of stillness and movement, the head being characteristically still, or comparatively so, and the limbs being characteristically in motion, or potentially so. Thus rhythm either appears as movement (the free movement of the limbs) curtailed to regularity, or it can be seen as stillness endowed with movement, albeit limited to pulsation.

A good reason for delaying the teaching of the adverb to Class 4, though it is by no means an iron-hard, dictatorial one, relates to the age we are considering. Just because of the twofold nature of the middle, the two are not always easy to distinguish. Consider the following phenomenon, for instance. When we hear someone's voice, say over the phone, do we distinguish that in its quality which is due to the person's vocal cords and organs, where the sound is *produced*, from that quality which is the result of the air pockets in the anatomy which *resonate* the sound, together with the stream of air which carries it? (As Wolfgang Schad pointed out in his research on 'the middle', production of sound and resonance represent a significant twofoldness in human nature.) If the ego is going to benefit from the strength of raising the pre-"I" attainment of grammar-informed-speech into awareness, it is clearly of importance that it (or its soul assistants) should be able to distinguish each of the grammar's component parts – not always a simple matter, in any case, in the English language. In order to achieve that clarity, the first examples of noun combined with verb that we introduce will most probably have avoided sentences such as

{Bakers bake.}
{Thatchers thatch.}
or even
{Prophets prophecy.}

though these can be fun, *for the children to invent*, too, once the relative organs of grammatical perception are firmly in place and sufficiently developed.

Further thought will shed light on the value of allowing the function of the *adjective* (with its Class 3 nomenclature) to be firmly grasped first before expecting the $9^{th}/10^{th}$ year novice in grammar know-how to be able to swing effortlessly between the two (middle-system-closely-related) parts of speech, adjective and *adverb* – the latter if introduced in Class 4, not needing pedagogically-geared nomenclature. And we must leave it to the linguistic conscience of the teacher as to whether – and if so, how – he/she decides to present the tempting etymological cocktail of *ad+verbum* which tickles the taste-buds uncannily like *add+verb*, to support her case. Leaving that aside, the class can now revel in rich sessions of grammatical train-spotting in which adjective and adverb in sentences such as the following can first be identified and then mimicked by the children in so-called creative writing:

Notes

{The clown tried desperately to prevent the huge bucket of water from spilling all over him, but tripped up clumsily over his floppily colossal boots at the last minute and got hopelessly drenched, much to the intense delight of the audience who rocked with explosive laughter.}.

Further, they might easily be able to advance to pigeon-holing (colour-coding) most of the words in sentences such as:

{[The] busy ploughman let [his] horses stand quietly.}

Notes

{[The] stone mason carefully selected [a] good strong piece [of] marble [for the] corner stone [of the] arch.}
{Moses bowed humbly [before the] burning bush.}
{[The] milkmaid sang sweetly [as she] poured out [the] fresh warm milk [into the] churn.}.

From the foregoing, it will come across that the ego at the Rubicon is the main keynote to take into consideration in Class 4. There is hardly anything that is more symptomatic of this than that pinprick of a word, the *preposition*.

When the soldiers left their base and crossed the Rubicon to face the oncoming foe they were acutely conscious of being cut off from their own city by the uncrossable stream, now at their backs. This is redolent of 9-year-old children who, in crossing over this climacteric bridge of life, experience their egos as being severed to whatever extent from their spiritual home. Correspondingly, the preposition expresses separation {in, beyond, above, from...}. However (to look at another feature of the year which has a similar resonance), just as the *round*, which is begun to be sung and played in Class 4, splits a melody by entering the second voice only after the first voice has sung its first phrase, *also* offers the otherwise unobtainable experience of two separate voices combining to form a harmonious relationship, so can the 10th-year child experience, as well as the *separateness* encapsulated in the preposition, the *relationship* equally implied by it:

{The friends sat beside one another enjoying the frisky pranks of the squirrels.}
{The bricklayer bonded the second course of bricks upon the first in such a way that bricks and mortar overlapped.}
{Once the hammer was in Thor's hands again, he threw off the bride's veil that had covered his bristling beard and thundered revenge on the giants.}
{A few blocks away from the school was the post box in which the children posted their business letters to the blacksmith whose forge they had recently visited at the far end of the next village.}
{As it galloped, the hooves of the whinnying horse hardly touched the ground as they hurled clods of earth into the air.}.

Notes

The *pronoun* is also a part of speech worth dwelling on in Class 4. The enhanced ego experience that comes with the Rubicon also ushers in an enhanced experience of other people's egos. This is the arena of the pronoun. All its cases can first be lumped in:

{Odin pointed to the herd of horses that were grazing there and bid him [Sigurd] drive them down the river's bank into the raging torrent.}
{The mouse could be heard in the loft sharpening its teeth.}
{"These thirds are for you," said Ernie to his sister as he unwrapped their pizza, "and this one is mine."}

Notes

{We went with our teacher to the top of the hill where she explained to us how our school had been built well above the flood plain.}
{Last week Group B started off their round with confidence but they hesitated where it came to the full bar's rest.}.

The newly-experienced ego of the 10-year-old can also be well affirmed through the local geography-cum-history (*Heimatkunde*) main-lesson, usually a great favourite, where the four points of the compass help with the child's spatial orientation. Similarly with time orientation. Hence, the verb which has been introduced as a part of speech in the previous year (in all its forms: *speak, spoke, spoken, speaks, speaking* for instance – and possibly even *spake* and *speakest* when savouring the style of the Old Testament) is now differentiated into the three main tenses of past, present and future. If the teacher can fit it into the year's schedule, it is well worth dedicating a separate main-lesson to this.

Class 4

The Verb in Relation to the Rubicon's Launch into Life

We have noted that the ego, as the fourth member of the human constitution, does not follow the septennial rhythm of its three sheaths: physical, etheric and astral. The strong affinity which *the verb* has with the Rubicon exemplifies this distinct quality of the ego, i.e. the spotlight it receives in the fourth class, being differentiated into past, present and future tenses, whereas the two other parts of speech introduced in the previous year (noun and adjective) are merely revised – always allowing, of course, for individual emphases that each class teacher may wish to give in accordance with her class's perceived needs, such as going more deeply into concrete nouns:

{roof, rooves, dog, [dog] collar, dog-collar, moon's},

abstract nouns:

{thankfulness, enthusiasm, honesty, alarm},

spiritual nouns:

{angel, saint, God, troll}

Notes

or proper nouns:

{Iduna, Londonderry, Thames, Scandinavia, Vikings, Cotswolds}.

And perhaps harvesting some grammatical finesse by making sentences which contain words having the same root but performing different parts of speech.

{The reapers celebrated harvest-home with a joyful barn dance.}
{Rabbits scurried hither and thither as the cornfield was reaped.}
{The honing of scythes and the swish of the barley as it gently fell onto the ground accompanied the welcome news that reaping time had arrived at last.}
{The undergraduates reaped the benefit of the hard work they had done during their three-year university course by getting good degrees.}
{As ye sow, so shall ye reap.}.

Such 'advance' may be considered irrelevant, optional or premature for Class 4 by many, and certainly not in the same category as those Waldorf curriculum topics which have come to be universally experienced as invariably supportive of child development. In this respect, if the involvement in the verb implied by its differentiation into the three main tenses tallies with the child's physiological or psychological development, one would expect it to be placed either in the first $2^{1/3rd}$ years sub-phase, between ages 7 and $9^{1/3rd}$ (following the general pattern of soul development: willing, feeling, thinking), or in the last $2^{1/3rd}$ years sub-phase, between ages $12^{2/3rds}$ and 14 (following the general pattern of bodily growth-spurts: head, trunk, limbs), yet neither of these is the case. We have already associated the three tenses with the ego's orientation in time. What are its other connections with this *doing* word? Let us look here at three: (i) the connection with what is representative of the essence of humanity, (ii) the connection with the age in which we live, and (iii) the connection with the mission of the earth.

Notes

On the first day of Class 1, if we follow Steiner's advice, we begin the first main-lesson with a conversation with the children in which we draw attention to their hands, that part of the body which is the ultimate link for what we do in life, whether we are peeling turnips, are part of a team constructing a space mission to Mars, 'penning' a haiku, or simply helping a friend on with their coat. With this 'message' concerning the human hand in the background, in Class 4, the main-lesson often referred to as 'man and animal', concentrates on the outer bodily form of the animal and its being a perfect 'tool' for its instinct:

{The tigress has powerful canine teeth for tearing the flesh from the carcass of the animal she has hunted.}

{The kingfisher's small, nimble body is headed by a long powerful beak, ideal for scooping up fish from near the surface of the river.}

{The pig thrust its solid snout and thick, muscular neck between two of the other sows to force its way to the trough.}.

The tigress's tooth, the kingfisher's long, pointed beak and the pig's snout may be seen as quasi 'limbs' whereby the animal instinctively preserves its life (and the 'survival of the fittest'), with the rest of their bodies ideally fashioned to serve the same purpose. How different from the human hand which is even embryonic by comparison, yet so subtly and flexibly formed that the human being may 'turn his hand' to anything. As it so happens, this age is often the point at which *modelling* in the Lower School classes – *the* artistic activity most intimately connected with the whole hand – takes a step forward both in content (modelling the animals that have been the focus of the Class 4 'man and animal' main-lesson), and in material (from the soft beeswax of the first class, via perhaps a clay that has been somewhat warmed through by including the 'clocks' of dandelions or groundsel, or the 'beard' of old man's beard, when it is pugged).

Clay is dug from the earth – not the heaviest but in some ways the earthiest of earth's minerals. This leads us conveniently to another aspect of the ego. The children are incarnating in the age of the Consciousness Soul – quite possibly in many cases for the first time. This means that the ego enters the physical body, and thence its physical earthly surroundings, in a deeper way than evolution has seen in former epochs. The shift in the drawing lesson from form drawing to that of drawing objects placed before the child supports this deeper incarnating of the ego, bringing sense perception to be focused on the outer physical object, in contrast to the inner feeling for form exercised in form drawing per se, practised in the years when the child was approaching the Rubicon. By the same token, and in connection with the grammatical task of the year, the teacher will be on the lookout for examples in the practical life of the local vicinity which she can describe vividly, in some cases perhaps following up with a visit, and which, apart from the children's own creatively written up versions of such experiences, she will herself lead the way by writing or dictating examples such as:

Notes

{Already as we approached the quarry, we could hear the ear-splitting shriek of the high-powered saw, cutting through the hard blocks of sandstone.}

{The fertility of the corn fields had been maintained over the centuries through the spreading of heaped cartloads of well-rotted manure, taken originally from the byres where the cattle had been wintered.}

{The bypass had been built, not only to skirt the old village, but on a route carefully surveyed to keep the gradient down to a minimum, which avoided the frequent pileup that had formerly been an annoying feature of village life in the severer winter months.}

{Despite the groins that had been built and the huge concrete blocks that had been deposited to protect the cliffs, the ruins of the coastguard's

Notes

cottage were a grim and permanent warning that even the towering chalk face, sun-drenched in all its white majesty, was no match for the relentless onslaught of the storm-churned breakers, foaming on the rock-strewn shore below, and their victorious booming in the caves that gaped at the foot of the promontory.}.

It is, of course, in their *will* that the inhabitants of a particular district have to contend with its topographical features, as far as their buildings and transport are concerned, and with the geological conditions of its topsoil, bedrock and mineral consistency, insofar as their subsistence and its economical implications are concerned. It can therefore be a boon for the strengthening of the ego-in-childhood, incarnating in the Consciousness Soul Age, if the teacher can lead the way in the child's written work by using vocabulary and syntax which harness verbs (in whatever form, participles included) that encapsulate the working dialogue between man's ordinary quotidian existence and the patch of earth where he lives it out.

Finally, as a kind of specialist branch of all the above, the study of the locality from the viewpoint of geography-cum-history gives the children an unparalleled opportunity to connect with the trades of a bygone age. A good mascot to follow is to be found in a verse such as the well-known Sussex alliterative poem from the Middle Ages, *Swart smirched smiths smattered with smoke, / Drive me to death with the din of their dents...* Half an hour spent with one's local phone directory may give some indi-

Notes

cation as to which trades were prominent in the district. How many Potters are listed? How many Turners, Tanners, Glovers, Millers, Ferriers, Boatmans, Wrights, Faulkners, Chapmans, Shepherds, Tailors, Chandlers, Cutlers, Coopers, Fletchers, Brewers, Smiths, Sawyers...? The list could go on, though there will always be the Margaret Thatchers who are ex-directory!

Tracing the whereabouts of the former workplaces of such people is one possibility; the children themselves might help build up the picture through enquiring of neighbours, particularly if they happen to be older inhabitants of the district. From the stories and anecdotes that result, written accounts can follow which incorporate some technical reference to trade practices, tools and processes:

{As the threshers 'rang the changes', they stood in their circle on the threshing floor, just as they stood on Sundays in the bell chamber at church, their hands clutching the dangling bell ropes and their hearts ringing with the song of the summer sun ripening the golden grain.}
{The farmer rejoiced to see the newborn lambs nuzzling beside their ewes, and thought what a splendid season lay ahead, with the much-needed income from the sheared fleeces he could expect.}
{As the baker finished kneading the last bin of dough he told his new apprentice: "It will take twenty minutes for the dough to rise, giving us just enough time to grease the baking tins."}.

Notes

Though many of such trades are what we associate with the rural life of earlier times, the same, or similar activities were to be found in the towns and cities. These were organised as guilds, where the inbred *morality* and *integrity* of the various trades-people and craftsmen was more regularised, so that true value, quality and an ethical attitude of service towards the community pervaded the economic life of society. This is a vitally important image to convey to the ego at the Rubicon, one which, with humanity as a whole having crossed an evolutionary Rubicon (from its more spiritual roots of earlier times to the more earth-bound – and therefore prone to material acquisitiveness – condition of the Consciousness Soul) which presents the danger of unethical practices, such as we see in the short change that is sadly not uncommon in the building trade or the scandalous behaviour of investment banking across the globe in recent years. Counter-images will therefore stand the ego in good stead:

{As well as paying the harvesters the wage agreed for their day's work, the good-natured farmer often sent them home with a pat of butter or a freshly baked pasty in their knapsacks, which swung from their scythes as they plodded wearily but happily on their homeward journey.}

{When the tailor had completed her winter coat, he gave his customer a soft warm blanket for her newborn baby, neatly sewn and hem-stitched from an off-cut from some fine woven cloth he had to hand.}

{His trugs and hurdles were widely known to be the best in the valley, the cottagers and shepherds more often than not bringing him some of their produce – a jar of cherry jam, a bunch of carrot thinnings, a few ounces of sheep cheese and so on – for his growing family.}.

Finally, it is good if the teacher bear in mind the spiritual reality behind *vocational* (manual) work. Whereas wisdom represents the fruit of seeds sown long ago in the history of humanity, the seeds represented by vocations which necessitate manual labour will bear fruit only in the far distant future. The story of the man who planted trees is an archetypal picture of this, in that he consciously labours not for himself but for those who will reap the reward of his industry when the trees are fully grown. It will also be good to tell the children of deeds that, while being equally of service for the future, do not take as long to 'mature' as it takes a forest to grow. Longer spans of time too, where possible. In the locality, while there may not be a Gothic cathedral, say, there will surely be some building – the town hall, the fire station, a war memorial, the library – that has served the community for some years, and the teacher will be able to go back to its original construction and what motivated the original owners, donors or share-holders, and from that perspective look to the present and, indeed, beyond to the still farther future.

Notes

Class 5

The Conjunction

The part of speech particularly akin to the child's changing consciousness in Class 5 is the *conjunction*. In English main-lessons and extra main-lessons, therefore, having re-worked to whatever extent is necessary the previous six parts of speech, it is beneficial to focus on conjunctions in the structure of sentences.

Stylistically conjunctions help the rampant-like use of and (and then... and then... etc.) often met with in the child's written accounts, say, of Greek myths, to be curtailed, and a more structured shape to result in the sentence. In the opposite direction, they help the clockwork-soldier, single-clause-sentence type of narrative to overcome its jerkiness and begin to flow:

{Despite the unforgettably powerful impression of the Giants Causeway's hexagonal columns of granite, the reappearance of the feature in the vast temple-like rock walls of Fingal's Cave off the coast of Scotland is nothing short of awe-inspiring.}

Notes

{Although the patient cow, ruminating in the buttercup-carpeted pasture, looks a picture of placidity itself, she can make well-aimed, bull-like use of her jutting horns if the occasion calls for it.}.

Technically, the conjunction is similar to the *preposition*: it is a word whose function is to join. Whereas the preposition tends to relate 'things' to their circumstances:

{One of the corks suddenly flew off the bottle of apple juice he was storing away for the winter.}
{The Channel Tunnel was drilled beneath the English Channel beginning a few miles south of Ashford.},

the conjunction is the ideal mental tool for joining *thoughts*, conveying further meaning, adding nuance, propelling the narrative forward:

{To this day, it is a mystery how the Ancient Egyptians, with only the primitive technology they had at their disposal compared with ours, built the great pyramid of Cheops and the similar though lesser pyramids that followed it in the third millennium BC.}
{It is one of the wonders of the world, though not in the traditional sense of the expression, that a regular hexagon fits beautifully into a circle whose radius is exactly the same as the side of the hexagon.}.

Notes

Psychologically, the function of the conjunction provides an endless supply of flowing 'water' to turn the mill wheel of "I look into the soul", at least as far as the thinking soul force is concerned:

{On second thoughts, however, the town council built the new housing estate even higher up from the flood plane than they had originally planned.}
{Evidently the drought, now in its third year, had spelt disaster for all the shallow-rooted plants.}.

Not only that, since the children are still essentially at the heart of the second septennial phase, the conjunction provides the perfect grammatical climate for their strong feeling life:

{But since Polyphemus roared, "No-one has blinded me," his neighbours retraced their footsteps, shrugging their shoulders and pulling odd-looking faces as they went back to their work places.}
{The intense silence that fell over the crowd as Alexander turned Bucephalus so that he faced the sun, however, erupted into a multitudinous shout of triumphant joy as the youth leapt onto the spirited creature's sweat-soaked back.}.

Looking at the word from a neurological viewpoint, it would appear to support that inner development of the child which is midwifed particularly through following Rudolf Steiner's recommendations for plant study [in his *Discussions with Teachers*]: to lead over from a sense-orientated description of the plant – e.g. the fern in its shade-loving, often dank-tending, moisture-assured environment – to the equivalent stage of development of the human being in childhood in which the consciousness is still bathed somewhat in the diffused light of dreaminess. This recommendation could be seen as one of the great menhirs guiding the teacher towards the stone-henge of Class 5, in which the child's etherically-born *picture thinking*, so methodically nourished through the narrative material in the first five years of the Lower School, and via which the child directly *learns* (just as adolescents and adults learn through exercising their faculty of rationality), is guided towards the world of *metaphor*. This is not the metaphor which is concealed in so many words in popular usage where changed consciousness over long periods of history has buried the original meaning to the extent of undiscoverability – the 'lady' was the 'loaf-kneader' of the household [see Owen Barfield: *A History in English Words*]; or where the original meaning takes second place to the extent of not being even noticeable – his display of courage was truly a *beacon* for the other mariners. It is that usage of metaphor which, whether gently, joltingly or roughly, pricks the consciousness into a degree of awareness, not dissimilar to how a lapidarist reveals a facet of a jewel's beauty that otherwise would have escaped attention. This, surely, apart from all the explicitly artistic activities in

Notes

Waldorf education, is a vital activity for the child approaching the threshold of early adolescence when those brain cells are eliminated which have not been myelinated, leaving the right hemisphere brain activity in jeopardy.

Every teacher will, of course, find her own creative application of the above, leading the child's use of language into this rich realm. Amongst her approaches may be:

1. her conscious use of conjunctions in her exposition-of-new-material part of the main-lesson (just as she has used relative clauses in earlier classes to encourage the etheric body's strength of flow);

2. similarly, her use of conjunctions in written material which she may decide either to dictate, or allow the children to copy from the board in the 'will section' of the main-lesson, using a method in which she engages the class (even as they copy) in her own creatively written version of the episode of the story – or other content – being 'written up;

3. her giving lead phrases for the class to complete in English lessons per se, which contain conjunctions.

{Even though the house had recently been double glazed, the sudden drop in temperature…}

{Many toadstools are edible; nevertheless…};

Notes

4. the simple exercise of fusing two separate sentences into one by the use of a conjunction.

{The tide having gone out, they were about to leave as planned to search for fossils, but as it started raining heavily they had to change into wellingtons and rain-proofs.};

5. her giving a short list of very familiar conjunctions

{and, but, because, however}

and less familiar ones

{since, despite, although, notwithstanding}

and asking the children to make a story in which some of them are used – based, perhaps, on a situation she may have outlined descriptively so that the child's 'middle realm' is engaged;

6. while taking utmost care not to lame the enjoyment of a story in a class reading-aloud session, pausing to ask the children what were the conjunctions in the sentence one of the children had just read out aloud:

{At that, Zeus thundered revenge and chained Prometheus to an exposed rock, which jutted out high up in the Caucasus Mountains.};

7. and finally, her keeping a watch on herself so that, although conjunctions have so much to offer the children at this stage in their development, all the same she should not allow the thin end of the intellectual wedge to insert itself into this otherwise pedagogically fruitful Class 5 (and upwards) grammatically adventurous topic.

Note:
Even if the teacher has introduced conjunctions at an earlier age, so that this Class 5 approach is already the children's second meeting with the part of speech, she may still consider it wise to delay looking at the three categories which classify conjunctions as subordinating, or coordinating, or correlative. It is the function of *joining* which accords with and which enriches the soul life at this stage that should be given priority. Nevertheless, if she decides to stop short of categorising, it obviously does not prevent the *usage* of all three categories of conjunction, albeit without going into their differentiation. On the contrary, it chimes harmoniously with the Waldorf principle of following that aspect of child development in which *understanding follows only after will-usage* – and in grammar teaching this principle lies at the heart of the pedagogical benefit that Steiner attributed to the subject.

Class 5

The Conditional

From introducing the children to the function of the part of speech we refer to as verb in Class 3, (usually following noun, the 'thing-word' which designates outer objects or inner perceptions), where the child realises that the function of the 'doing-word' in the sentence leads far from the pinning-down, pin-pointing, tunnel-vision-directed exactitude of its main partner in the sentence, we stride in Class 4 into the all-encompassing dimensions of *past, present and future* and then, in Class 5, leap into the orbital wonder that the soul experiences and expresses through pretty well the whole verb-ecliptic within the cosmos of grammar in human language. The frequently adopted Class 3 nomenclature for verb, 'doing-word', clearly connects the verb with the will. With conjunctions we saw that, though the content of the meaning that the conjunction links up may relate to the whole gamut of the soul forces – thinking, feeling and willing – it is principally through the mental awareness of the need to link up content that the speaker or writer has recourse to the conjunction as a reef-knotting-together grammatical device. The wealth of all the tenses (not yet subjunctive, though that is to come) and 'voices' of the verb provides a polaric balance

Notes

to that sharpening of mental awareness.

The *conditional* involves using an auxiliary verb – *may, shall* or *ought* – in one conjugation or another. This touches on an aspect of human development that is also reflected in Class 5 arithmetic in which from the always-precise number realm of fractions (3/8, 2/3) the children move into that number realm which enters into irrationality – 3/8 expressed as a decimal is precise (0.375), whereas 2/3 cannot be expressed as a decimal in precise terms ('point six recurring'); and we are on the road to the decimal merry-go-round of terms like π or $\sqrt{2}$. The ego, having been affirmed in its new post-Rubicon state through the work of Class 4, now faces uncertainty – objective uncertainty in arithmetic and subjective uncertainty (i.e. where freedom plays in) in the inner world expressed by terms such as *might've, shouldn't, didn't ought* etc. There is a world of difference between the Mosaic "Thou shalt not bear false witness," which leaves no leeway, and "He should have known better."

There is, of course, an outer application of may, shall and ought:

{It may well be that more Greek sculptures are still waiting to be discovered on the bed of the Adriatic.}
{The lion population of the Savannah should be able to maintain the balance in nature.}
{The enquiry concluded that the oil rig ought to have been strong enough not to collapse.}.

Notes

Whilst entering such areas of conditional uncertainty, however, the children also need to be led into the soul's own fallibility / vulnerability:

{It may be that the self-regulation of the fishing industry will be sufficient to preserve the shoals of cod in the North Sea, but I have my doubts.}
{Many people from different walks of society consider that there ought to have been much more consultation before giving the go-ahead to build a high speed railway track through the very heart of the Chilterns, some of the most beautiful countryside in the south-east.}
{Ornithologists should surely have realised that they were endangering the future of the osprey by collecting its eggs in the region where it had only just started once more to breed.}
{"If only Euridice could be restored to me," lamented Orpheus as he journeyed far and wide in his distress.}.

On the one hand, there is the world of outer physical reality which is subject to condition (not just the weather!); on the other hand there is the inmost world of the ego in which morality dwells, where the human condition can be either at its strongest or its weakest. Even a modest dictionary such as *The Concise Oxford Dictionary* goes into comparatively great length in order to convey the facets of meaning connected with *may, shall* and *ought*, all of which is rooted in concepts related to conscience. It is something of a strange anomaly, incidentally, that we use a Classically-derived word,

Notes

conscience, for that inner 'voice' for which languages / peoples much more closely allied to 'Rome' – Portuguese, Spanish, Italian, French, for example – do not include in their vocabulary a word that differentiates it markedly from consciousness! This observation provides a convenient stepping stone to the next consideration of grammar in the fifth class: 'voices' of the verb.

Class 5

'Voices' of Verbs

In the new morning verse spoken at the beginning of each day in Classes 5-12, the second stanza contains the line, "In light of sun and soul." Via the perspective of the *conditional* tense, we have seen how the 'light of sun' illumines facets of both the outer and inner worlds, and in particular the world of morality and the voice of human conscience that prompts our ability to hear what is of moral value – or its opposite. In an age in which that soul force which rightly should be paramount in the third septennial phase, thinking, has tended to overshadow, if not obliterate, the value of the rightful regents of the first and second septennial phases, willing and feeling, we are inclined to lose sight of other vital elements in the development of the child. It is even possible that the term Middle School, which has crept into popular parlance in some Waldorf environments, is a symptom of that obfuscating of what were the essentials. (For Steiner, Lower School – *Unterstufe* – and Upper School – *Oberstufe* – sufficed.)

A further consideration of conscience and its relationship to karma may help to restore that confidence which Steiner had in maintaining the overall integrity of the septennial phases – the second one in particular – and ensuring that the shares of

Notes

the intellect that have rocketed on the stock market of consciousness during the twentieth century do not blind us to the value of other aspects in human nature. For it is during the years of puberty that the question of karma – in the sense: When do I become karmically responsible for my own deeds? – begin to well up from the depths of the soul. A schooling of consciousness is manifestly important as a psychological hinterland for this vital port of embarkation from which the ego eventually sails out upon the open ocean of life.

There are two ramifications of the 'voices' of verbs experienced in Class 5, which have direct bearing on this, ramifications which can be likened to the *light of soul* as complementary to the 'light of sun' considered above. They are (i) the schooled awareness of ego; and (ii) the becoming conscious of the two states signified by *being* and *having*. The first is aided by the way certain aspects of the 'voices' of verbs cultivate the higher senses, particularly those of 'word', 'thought' and (the other person's) 'ego'. The second leads into an awareness of auxiliary and main verbs in a clause or sentence.

In what is often one of the first ports of call for grammar in Class 5, in which the two-fold, complemental nature of the voices of verbs is reflected, the sense of ego is enhanced, albeit at an elementary level, through studying *direct and indirect speech*:

{The coal miner remarked that living so close to vocational danger was something that had always been part of family life.}

{Breathing the fumes issuing from the Python's cleft in the temple floor, the Delphic Oracle uttered, " … ".}.

The human condition is one in which, through the Luciferic Fall, the ego member strikes into the child's development step by step, earlier than the 'divine plan' had laid out. Following the Rubicon (one of the most characteristic of the ego's steps) and its often overwhelmingly conscious experience of *self*, the carefully cultivated awareness of the other's ego (the highest of the 12 senses) which an immersion into direct and indirect speech supports – and the modulation of the verb which moving from one to the other necessitates, not to mention the fun and fuss of quotation marks and their attendant other punctuation, which give the children plenty to relish and get their grammatical teeth into – reflects in the soul. 'That is his or her ego that I perceive, the most sacred (in some respects) human entity: so it can be consciously investigated and cultivated in myself, too,' or words and feelings to that effect.

{It was as if the words inscribed over the entrance to Apollo's temple precincts called incisively to the neophyte, "Know thyself".}

In the concepts *being* and *having* may be seen embodied the two states of what the human being *is* (that which unfolds from the depths of the karmic past) and what the human being acquires, and thus *has*, (that which life endows in the present incarnation). In this connection, it is particularly noteworthy that *to be* and *to have* comprise

Notes

the two most common *auxiliary verbs*. Thus, although in the grammar lesson these two auxiliary verbs will most likely mainly be applied to externalities:

{The rising of the star Sothis was awaited with great anticipation, since, for their subsistence the Egyptians depended on the flooding of the Nile, by which its rising was usually accompanied.}
{Having flushed out the china clay from the pockets of the granite in which it has been deposited, through the use of water hosed at high pressure, the valuable mineral then has to be further extracted from the resultant slurry by a process of distillation. Any one who has travelled in the area of St Austell will have seen the mounds of white clay which have dominated the landscape for centuries.},

in using a biographical story as a stepping stone, however, opportunities may well arise, which enable the children also to look inward – not, needless to say, in an indulgent way:

{St Francis, it seemed, was fortunate to have inherited an affluent life-style from his well-to-do family, but a life-changing moment came when, supported by the Bishop of Assisi, he gave all he had, including the clothes on his back, back to his father.}.

Let us continue to explore how the three *higher* senses may be particularly illumined by exercises in the *voices of verbs*. For example, whether a verb is finite or non-finite (as in its participles or the *infinitive* itself), is a feature of grammar that the children will have been masters of in their personal use of language for years, and it may give impetus to our aim in grammar teaching if the teacher reminds herself of the principle at stake (first stated in 'Why Grammar?') and its implications for the child's incarnating ego. In order to school the awareness of the ego's inner life, examples of *finite / non-finite* verbs can be practised in extra main-lessons and sprinkled richly through the oral and written sections of main-lessons themselves. In the sentence

{His thoughts went back to the days when, following his family's seasonal cycle of work, he ran bare foot in the Kent countryside, playing with the other workers' children and sleeping under the stars at the edge of the fields where his father and mother had been hop-picking from dawn till dusk.}

there is an example of how, in a 'creative writing' exercise, the several phrases in the sentence call upon the *sense of thought* to combine all the components into the full picture. From there it can lead, as if going through an open door, into a world, imagined through the teacher's description the previous day, but nevertheless a reflection of real conditions of times not so long ago when life was different.

Or the teacher may school the children's *sense of word*. One scenario might be that she pauses during the written-up recall of the battle of Salamis that she and the class are composing together:

Notes

{"Children: Instead of simply writing, 'The Greeks' courage quaked as they saw the massive Asiatic ships, but Themistocles, feeling sure that the mobility of the Greek fleet would win the day said, ...' what shall we write?" – and then pupils are encouraged to be forthcoming with expressions to replace the bland 'said', so that the urgency of the hour is embodied in the choice of vocabulary.}.

There will be such opportunities virtually every day of school. As well as this, the teacher will be on the look out for jogging the still higher *sense of thought*, perhaps by deepening something she has related in class when it comes to the written form, or by juxtaposing thought-prompting facts:

{On the one hand, the Greek gods and goddesses were portrayed in idealised human form, as seen in the superb marble sculptures that stood towering above in the tympanum of the temple. On the other hand, their behaviour as recounted in the Greek myths, unless it is interpreted as the philosophers did, does not by any means always resemble human behaviour.}.

All 'partnered' voices of the verb – *finite and non-finite, active and passive, transitive and intransitive, main and auxiliary, continuous and definite* – offer abundant opportunity to develop the pupils' sense of style, so that the eventual study in different artistic genres in the Upper School has a good foundation on which to draw, laid down during the second septennial phase through pure 'doing' – undistracted by explanation or conscious analysis. This is not to say that content, which is later studied in detail (as in the following examples that refer to content that may be revisited in Classes 8 and/or 9), cannot be glimpsed in a Class 5 context.

Notes

With this in mind, the examples which follow are derived from exercises in the use of *active* and *passive*, and touch on themes met in the geography of the British Isles:

{It was William Wilberforce who worked tirelessly throughout his parliamentary life, and finally succeeded in getting the law changed so that slaves were protected from being traded by the unscrupulous capitalists of the great 'slave-trading triangle', one corner of which was focused in ports like Bristol and Liverpool.}.

En passant, it may be of value to mention that this sentence embodies my belief that, once a topic such as this has been introduced, the accounts written up in main-lesson books (the Waldorf equivalent of the text book) should make inner demands of various kinds e.g. when the children re-read them or when they take a later look at a page that contains an illustration or diagram:

{The ships with their cargoes plied the east coast, taking the coal from Newcastle to London, a trade which gradually ousted many of the older ways of life.}

Notes

{St Bride landed on the Isle of Iona in the Hebrides from where Celtic Christianity streamed across the north of the mainland.}
{Many museums exhibit Roman copies of Greek sculpture, that were originally brought across the Adriatic.}.

To conclude, let us savour examples of other complementary voices, which could feature alongside or during the geography, eagle-lion-bull or history main-lessons of the year:

{Growing in the pure air of the mountains, gives many of the so-called alpines their medicinal value – ***finite / non-finite*****}**
{To load his little pony and cart with seaweed for manuring his potato patch within the sound of the churning shingle, thrilled the crofter in his very being – ***finite / non-finite*****}**
{Although the audience at Epidaurus was so vast, you could hear the smallest stage whisper wherever you sat – ***main / auxiliary*****}**
{The foundry at Loughborough is where bells are still being cast – ***main / auxiliary*****}**
{Just as the vast herds of ungulates that graze on the plains of central Africa are regulated by the lion – in its traditional role as 'king of the jungle' – so we can recognise occasions in life when an impulsive action is tempered by our gut feeling – ***active / passive*****}**

{They pulled up by the oak and gathered mistletoe for the festival – *transitive / intranstive*}

{Many hikers visit High Force which is one of the most impressive features of the Great Whin Sill in the north of England – *transitive / intransitive*}

{Like an eagle soaring in the heights, we struggle with a problem until it is solved – *continuous / definite*}

{The spirit of darkness, Ahriman, sought to slay Zarathustra at his birth; but he failed, and the great leader of the Persians grew up to direct his people in how they should conduct their lives. As they ploughed the land, its fertility was maintained; through tolerating the wolf, the animal became tame and protected the sheep which it had formerly preyed upon – *continuous / definite*}.

Notes

Notes

Class 6

The Article

The degree to which the article appears in various languages varies. Where the declension of a noun says it all, as in Latin, for instance, it is implied but not present as a word in the sentence: *Hodie puer natus est*, says the old chant. It is as if the grammar moves in uninhibited watery currents – though these do have their laws. Even more liberated, the chameleon-like grammatical basis of Slav languages, seems to result in a folk psychology that is baffled by the article. Someone whose native tongue is of Slav derivation is used to the 'free air' that blows in the inflections of the language. But in English, and in the sequence of parts of speech that is being followed here, it is as vital as feet are for those who walk on land. The image of the Grimms' 'The Golden Goose' comes to mind, where the thief who has stolen the goose becomes stuck to those he beseeches to help him get free: in grammatical terms, noun, verb, adjective, adverb, pronoun, preposition, conjunction and (now) article, tagging on at the end. However, the 'tagging on' by no means implies inferiority.

This can be seen if we examine the symbiosis between the *article* and some of the core elements in the curriculum in Class 6.

The term *article* is derived from the word meaning 'joint'. From this point of view it follows the process we saw in the sequence: preposition – conjunction, i.e. having a linking function in the sentence. However, where prepositions indicate relationships of objects (beside, beyond, in front of ...), and where conjunctions link the thinking process of the speaker / writer (not only that, whereas, in spite of …), the article – joined to the noun (or the verb in its gerundive form) – leans more towards the separateness, the identity, the distinctiveness of that to which it is joined than the notion of joining might suggest:

Notes

{The lemming regulates its population by migrating to the coast in droves and throwing itself to its death over the cliffs into the sea.}
{Caligula, the notorious Roman Emperor, sometimes dressed in a lion's skin, holding a club in his hand, and was revered as Hercules, considering himself to be as an equal among the ranks of the gods.}
{In at least one of the great medieval cities, the Guild of Mercers was responsible for presenting the *Three Kings Play* in the Corpus Christi pageant, providing costly material for the robes of Melchior, Balthazar and Caspar.}.

The carpenter's joint – dovetail, mortice and tenon etc. – joins two rigid structures together in such a way that the final result – a cupboard drawer, a window frame, a roof joist – is also rigid. Joints in the skeleton of animals enable movement, but are in themselves so wonderfully 'engineered' that the elephant can carry its weight while walking (even charging!), that the jaguar can speed across the ground, and that the human being can move fully from the upright position and with the upper limbs particularly in an incredibly free way.

The German language reflects, in its preponderance of articles, the pensively structured nature of the speaker's thought life. Indeed, this is further emphasised by the nouns (subjects, objects and indirect objects) often being placed, like men on a chess board, at the beginning of the sentence – followed by the verb which reveals how the thinking-speaker moves the chess pieces:

{*Der Kaiser hat dem Oberstleutnant einen Befehl gegeben.* The emperor gave the colonel a command.}.

At the other end of the scale, when toddlers first begin to speak, it would be surprising to hear an article: "Me more porridge," suffices. The toddler's still supple and somewhat cartilaginous joints tally tellingly with its article-less, swimming grammar structure. Rudolf Steiner suggested that the title of his seminal book *Die Pholosophie der Freiheit* be translated as *The Philosophy of Spiritual Activity* (authorising, so to speak, the loss of one article!). Subsequent translators have dared to drop the other article – not uncommon in titles, in any case – resulting in *Philosophy of Freedom*.

Against this background, may be placed the stage of child development at age 12. Although the methodology of teaching subjects such as history and geography ideally should emphasise the descriptive rather than the rational, elsewhere in the curriculum that which is akin to structure in grammar (epitomised in the present context by *the article*) indicates that a vital step is taking place in the child's thought structure, which begins to move in the direction of the third septennial phase: deductive geometry, percentages and ratio in arithmetic, the Goethean phenomenological approach to science, more 'organised' sports (though avoiding the tendency to plunge into the slough of Philistinism), a more conscious application of the colour circle in painting and an increasing awareness of the rudiments of music theory embodied in the songs and part songs they are singing and in the pieces they are playing both solo and in various combinations of instrumental ensembles.

Though greatly contrasted to how the heavenly constellations were experienced in ancient times by people who enjoyed a markedly different form of consciousness, it might help the appreciation of the article in the sentence (and thus help school the sense of thought) if one associates the other parts of speech – nouns, adjectives, verbs, etc. – with the stars which define the gesture of the sentence's thought forms, and the articles as the straight lines which join the starry points of illustration (as in modern depictions of the constellations), making visible to the apprehending mind the otherwise only suggested shape. The following examples have no less than 8, 13 and 9 articles respectively:

Notes

{The below-sea-level polder provides the ideal conditions for the moisture-loving pasture on which the renowned Frisian milking herds graze, and for the cultivation of the many varieties of tulips for which the Dutch have become leaders in the world.}

{In long boats, for which they were famous, the intrepid Norsemen sailed across the North Sea, raiding the crops and cattle belonging to the dwellers who lived round the coasts of the British Isles and the north-western part of Europe, sometimes also mingling with the local inhabitants to form the Viking colonies which are among the ancestors of the population today of Normandy, the Isle of Man, the Ridings of Yorkshire and elsewhere.}

{The Romans' policy in religious matters was usually to bring the deities of the peoples they conquered, in the expansion of the empire, into their Olympus, but the Senate frustrated Tiberius' wish to place the god of the Christians alongside all the others.}.

This is not the technique of introducing clauses that Steiner recommends for Class 8, but it may be a helpful factor in bridging the 'picture thinking' that was prevalent in the earlier classes (as a recapitulatory manifestation of the 'original participation' that pervaded the consciousness of earlier civilisations) to that form of thinking we principally exercise as modern, rational adults.

Such considerations are the 'stuff' of the article as a part of speech, and is the core function it serves in sentence construction, which the children need to grasp strongly and feel appreciatively as part of the whole process of 'lifting' unconscious grammar *usage* of the mother tongue into conscious *awareness*: the gift of grammar teaching to the incarnating ego as a source of inner strength. Whether the teacher also feels the time is ripe for further subtleties – and if so, to what extent – must be at her own discretion. They are not necessarily vital in the Lower School. They could, however, be touched on in extra English main-lessons or deferred until a later class.

Some of these subtleties are categorised as follows. The use of the article:

a) to denote something that exists, whether actually or potentially:

{Out of the city's hitherto fortified gates, *the burghers of Calais* slowly strode, with the utmost dignity yet chained to one another in line, towards where the king waited to pronounce their fate.}

{*The sacred stone* was restored to its resting place in Scone.};

b) to denote something that is recognised widely as unique:

{*The Fire of London* raced through the city leaving black devastation in its wake.}

{*The Baptist*, who fully immersed his followers in Jordan when they received baptism, would call out, "Repent, for the Kingdom of Heaven is at hand."};

Notes

c) to denote something that is familiar, either personally or more usually in the public domain:

{*The ravens* strutted at the entrance to the Tower as the prisoner, bound and gagged, was led in.}

{With fish-farming on the increase, the responsible cultivation of salmon is moving towards a promising recovery of *the wild species*.};

d) to indicate something that is identifiable:

{In the distance the proud structure of *the Forth Bridge* came into view.}

{The châteaux of *the Loire Valley* are famed for the distinctive flavour of the wine that comes from their vineyards.}

{*The Palladium* was taken over to Rome and buried beneath a pillar of porphyry.};

e) to denote a species or type:

{*The gondolier* is one of the hallmarks of Venice, and the tourists' hopes were satisfied when they saw Giuseppe leap with elegant agility onto the steps which led from the Grand Canal to the palazzo where the reception was to take place.}

{He put away his tools as he finished making his last arrow, full of satisfaction that another day's work had been accomplished, and in no doubt that *the fletcher* was amongst the foundation stones of society.};

f) to denote a class or group:

Notes

{Bernard's powerful preaching resulted in more and more of *the wealthy nobles* joining the Crusades.}

{In full view of *the thousands of spectators*, instead of making a mockery of Christian baptism as planned, Gelasinus rose from out of the water and proclaimed: "I have now become Christian and shall defend Christianity with all the forces of my soul."}

{A large portion of *the dense population in the Ruhr Gebiet* is employed in heavy industry.};

g) to denote an occupation or pursuit:

{Sitting at their doorsteps in the spring sunshine, *the lace-makers* were at work, busily shifting their bobbins to and fro, like mosquitoes skimming above the surface of the canal below, to produce the exquisite patterns for which Bruges was famed in all the courts of the Middle Ages and the Renaissance.};

h) to refer to a disease of some kind:

{Each day *the plague* struck yet another household.}

{*The epidemic* struck again, spreading disaster to the regions where the cattle had been fed unwisely on certain protein.};

Notes

i) to denote a noun that is only completely comprehensible when followed by an adjective or clause:

{*The light that shone around the sword* convinced him that it was indeed Excalibur.}

{*The herrings, once oak-smoked in the sheds at Craster*, were deemed to be the best in the land.};

m) to draw attention to things related to one another:

{In his mad obsession, Philip the Fair exulted in the Templars' seized riches: thrusting his elbows into the heap of gold coins, '*the more the better*' swept through his acquisitive soul, like a rushing tornado.}

{*The more carefully* the farmer pruned his cork trees *the better* he was able to supply the trade with the prized Portuguese commodity.}.

Class 6

The Subjunctive

So rarely does the man in the street use the *subjunctive* tense of the verb in modern everyday English, that its existence can come as a surprise to children at this age (Class 6, age 12).

{**Unless *it rain* tomorrow, we shall go to the sea for the day.**}

and similar sentences more often than not get soaked with an auxiliary verb:

{**Unless it *should rain* tomorrow etc.**}

and the grammatical spark that the subjunctive can ignite in the soul goes completely damp-squibbed. "Oh that it were otherwise," you may think (assuming a familiarity with the subjunctive). But the general descent of culture is, for the most part, too powerful to resist or halt. Nevertheless, this is no argument for depriving the extending tentacles of the awakening pre-adolescent of the very special mental poise that it embodies. At the very least, it can be savoured as an archaicism, and if maybe once, or once-and-a-half in a blue moon, it come in handy, then that is a bonus!

Notes

Notwithstanding the everyday occurrence of phrases such as 'God help you,' 'If I were you,' 'Be that as it may,' or 'Suffice it to say' – where, in the last two, the subjunctive mood of the verb is less important than the conjunction-like function of the phrase as a whole – the argument that the subjunctive is so much at the fringe of grammatical usage that its immersion in a systematic teaching of the subject is neither here nor there, overlooks an important facet of child development. Let us revisit those topics in the Class 6 curriculum that have bearing on the gradual shift of the child's consciousness from a pictorial mode of thinking to one that is more rationally informed. We saw earlier a sequence from fractions to decimals (Classes 4 to 5) by which the mind is led from clearly outlined reality (2/3) to a mathematical realm in which number appears blurred if looked at through the microscope of decimal fractions ('point six recurring'). In the Class 6 topics of percentages and ratio (often also the rate of exchange from one currency to another) we 'lift' the cardinal reality of some entity (a bank deposit of, say, £60,000.00) into a theoretical realm by applying a percentage rate of interest to it, and a length of time (per annum), in order to calculate the actual interest that is payable to the depositor. The gambler indulges even further in the realm of theoretical uncertainty.

The conscious entry into the mood of the subjunctive, enables the mind to live as comfortably in this uncertain realm (not just in respect of number) as in the world of buttered toast or stalactites. Pliny recounts how, on seeing the vast Persian army camped in readiness for battle the next day, one of Alexander the Great's senior officers

Notes

has the temerity to sidle up to him and offer, "If I were you, I would attack at night and steal the victory." Without hesitation, Alexander's reply comes boomeranging back: "If I were *you*, I would *steal* the victory." Needless to say, such courage and divine certainty in his mission *won* the victory the next day!

We are back to the cliché 'if I were you', but with a difference. This anecdote removes the veil of unconscious casualness that usually accompanies clichés, to reveal an enhanced consciousness: that of Alexander's. It is such enhancement that is of value to the mind-advancing consciousness of the 12-year-old. For example:

{The harbour master reckoned that if the temperature drop still further, ice would begin to form on the surface.}
{Everything will be fine provided the lion tamer keep his nerve.}
{Lest the expedition take longer than planned, they decided to carry extra rations that would see them through.}.

It is not, of course, that, having seen the value of introducing the subjunctive, the teacher expects or hopes that the subjunctive occur in every other paragraph of the pupil's writing – though this can sometimes happen in rare cases where the experience of its mood has been savoured with such mental refreshment by a certain pupil that it becomes the flavour of the month.

And to conclude on a seriously light-hearted, slightly but acceptably-for-12-year-olds' irreverent, note, most English children enjoy discovering that in the coronation ritual shout of 'God save the queen', (a) God (the omnipotent!) is revealed only as *third* person singular; and (b) the verb 'save' indicates that the queen – in former times regarded as the representative in earthly society of that Divine omnipotence – cannot sit back resting on her laurels, since doubt lingers where what would otherwise be straightforward present tense (God saves the queen) or future tense (God will save the queen) and is replaced by the subjunctive *save*!

Class 7

Notes

Wish, Wonder, Surprise

There being no time or space in Spirit Worlds, as the ego experiences them after being born into a physical body on earth, the contrast in the two states of existence represents the crossing of thresholds. Three thresholds, in fact, in that the ego itself as experienced in daily life on earth is a threshold removed, so to speak, from that eternal entelechy to which we refer as the higher ego, investing it with that spiritual power which manifests again and again as the individual human being's mission within earth evolution.

This threefold 'crossing', which each newborn child undergoes, is experienced, it goes without saying, in a state of consciousness akin to sleep. It may not seem like that if we are woken as parents in the middle of the night by the child exercising its healthy newly-air-borne lungs, telling us in no uncertain terms that the newly acquired physical body is racked with hunger or discomfort! However, even the workaday ego, with which we travel through life, is basically as little connected with its brand new, workaday, tiny, physical-body strength, as is the case when in sound sleep, that consciousness of the discomfort – or, indeed, of the comfort that may ensue after the problem-solving nappy change, or the 'meal' of mother's milk – does not register. In fact, it hardly comes into question any more than it does when the adult's eyelid blinks as the result of that reflex which ensures that the eyeball gets its necessary mini-bathe, without which we would become conscious of discomfort.

At the human being's second 'birth', when passing from the first to the second septennial phase, the prevailing consciousness of childhood has passed from that which is related to sleep to something of a day-dreaming nature. With their full attention, albeit of a day-dreamy nature, we lift the three-threshold-crossing, that took place purely existentially at the outset of the first septennial phase, into the new region of awareness that dawns at c.7 years, by telling stories that are pregnant with images of the three thresholds, which the children can access with their newly acquired picture-thinking. These stories fall into three categories: the fairy story, the so-called nature story and the pedagogical story.

Whilst the great mythologies of different peoples could be said to recall the past, the *fairy story* – arising from the similar, imaginative (super-sensible) consciousness of an earlier time in history – tells of the present, but against the vast alpha-to-omega sweep of evolution. Hearing it, the child's imaginative consciousness is reminded of that threshold it crossed at birth which led into earthly time, the time we have available, as it were, to bring our impulse into the stream of earthly evolution – with all the potential pluses and minuses in our nature portrayed by the princes and dragons, the witches and queens, the forests and sea-shores, the ants and bees, the

Red-Riding Hoods and Goose Girls etc. that are strands in the myriad-minded motley of human nature that the gods have pinned their hopes on, that, conquering the long-term cosmically historical situation we may join their hierarchical ranks at some distantly future time, in tenth place.

And the 'stage' for this? Nothing less than the entire globe itself. However, we do not dwell in its richly different habitats all at once. Like Magellan, we sail full circle around it with each incarnation necessitating a new port of call. Unlike Magellan, at the same time, our voyage is not earthly but cosmic, the sequence of 'ports' depending on factors other than what follows naturally in terms of nautical miles, say from Cape Town to Port Elizabeth to Mombasa etc. Nevertheless each incarnation asks that the ego find its best environment for that element of its mission which needs to find fulfilment. A Michelangelo incarnating in Texas in the fifteenth century is manifestly an incongruity. The *nature story*, in which the ego is encouraged to become rooted in its home surroundings, confirms the fact that crossing the threshold from a spiritual, between-death-and-rebirth existence into earthly space, with its latitude and longitude, its hills and plains, its spring and autumn foliage, its tundra or tropical climate etc. leads to a vital port of call for that particular incarnation.

The *pedagogical story* raises an awareness of the third threshold crossed at birth from sleep- to day-dream-consciousness. In the pedagogical story the higher ego which guards the mission of the individual, so to speak, is invoked if difficult psychological circumstances are proving something of a chronic hindrance for the day-to-day ego to cope with, either directly or with the normal jollying along that children get from the adult environment in which they are socially integrated. Children too, of course, can be strangely effective at rubbing corners off one another. But the infallibility that each one of us carries, whether occultly pianissimo or blatantly obvious may well resist the corner-rubbing corrections of life's business-as-usual jostling... and, hey presto, the pedagogical story is brought into play. The teacher dives down to her sunken galley of bullion and brings to the surface whatever pedagogical insight she can find, trusting that when she surfaces again she will breathe the air of the child's higher ego and that the child's subservient ego forces follow suit and will do the same.

Finally – finally in the present context and from the point of view of a child's school life – the third, astral birth approaches and the 13/14-year-old's lingering picture-consciousness and strong feeling life are imbued with day-wakefulness. The waters of the river of childhood, tumbling from the heights and happily meandering across the plains of sleep-dreaminess begin to mingle with the salt of awakening consciousness as the river's estuary meets the incoming tide of the ocean of pubescent maturity and eventual adult responsibility. The Magellan of the first and second septennial phases, retires in favour of the Captain of the Soul, and that captain requires a chart of the soul's landscapes that will be discovered in the third septennial phase. Moreover, the more detailed the chart, the more serviceable it will be for the exploitation of the soul's three continents: the continent of thorn-threatened, fancy-tickled, fig-leaf-seeking, bumptiousness-reliant, self-conscious awareness; the continent of heart-true, horizon-widening, enquiry; and the continent of stars-at-twilight aspiration. We beach, wade through the shallows, kneel in thankfulness and then set foot in these three landscapes firstly in the Class 7 main-lesson *Wish, Wonder and Surprise* and with what we have discovered there in what follows in the evolving soul's life experience thereafter.

Though Richard II replies to the dying Gaunt's admonishing, "The stars are our heads": "I know it Uncle," his lack of putting his knowing into action that would redeem his profligacy in the eyes of his subjects, costs him his crown and life – first in the surprise of Bolingbroke's landing on English soil, thus defying his banishment, and second in the usurped throne that the victory of Bolingbroke's supporters virtually enforce. The presumed safety of a monarch's decree, the presumed safety of the British coastline, shrank into the presumed safety of Flint Castle, but then followed the inevitable, inexorable punctuating of it. *Surprise* is that element in life which punctures the soul's presumed inviolable castle walls – and of course it can be pleasant as well as unpleasant. The soul makes way for the dentist's anaesthetic needle inserted into the gum when he quietly (these days!) informs the patient of the forthcoming discomfort of the injection. Surprise has no truck with dental diplomacy. The air of surprise has happened – and hopped it – before you hear the bang of a burst balloon. In a mild form of surprise you are 'taken aback', or you raise your eyebrows, or you shrug your shoulders, depending perhaps on temperament; but in a severe form, surprise leaves you devastated, like the shrivelled balloon that has burst, or at the other extreme,

Notes

yippeeing with the rest of the grandstand when your rugby idol breaks through the opponent's defence unexpectedly and hurls himself down on the ball full length behind the goal posts.

How differently *wonder* works in the soul from the squall-from-nowhere, Jack-in-the-box suddenness of surprise. The great painting by Rembrandt of *Aristotle pondering the bust of Homer* says it all. With arm extended on Homer's marble brow, the philosopher mentally kedging his way forward, as he steers his rudder against the blowing-off-course winds that would disturb his thought, marvels at the visual torrents that surge unhesitatingly through the *Iliad* from the pen of a blind poet. It is, perhaps, pre-eminently wonder, that the silent world of sunrise, snow-capped mountain peak, sequoia forest, Niagara Falls, caraway seed, honey comb, distant galaxies, extinct dinosaur, uvarovite crystal, water expanding into ice, the engineering wisdom of a human femur, a cobra's poison, and all of nature's multi-million phenomena, begin to evoke. Whether it is the scientist wondering in her laboratory at a new strain of cancer, the beggar wondering where the next penny is coming from, Newton's supposed twin wondering how the apples got up the tree in the first place, or the despondent athlete wondering at the irrepressible joy of an MS sufferer confined to a wheel chair... the psychological process bears the same hall mark: the phenomenon that is the object of wonder and the inwardly active participation of the wonderer are in continuous flow, the opposite directions of which are not opposing but informing, enlightening, love- (in the best sense of the word) and profound interest-engendering.

Notes

When Milton in his 'Blest Pair of Sirens', having extolled the 'voice' and 'verse' which comprised the pair and recognised the divine world from which they emanate and which they reflect, turns his extolment towards the future that might lift the soul out of its sunken, harshly disjointed state, his upward yearning is launched with 'O', the sound of embrace. But it is not the rigid clamp of the Medieval stocks or the handcuff of a Hollywood cop; it is that part of the embrace which is just beginning its encircling arm gesture, so to speak: "O may we soon again renew that song." The interjection may also express surprise or wonder, of course ("Oh really!" "Oh, just look at this!") but its use by poets to express some degree of *wish* – wishing to find a way out of an existential dilemma, wishing to feel a touch of the ineffable or, most archetypally perhaps, the Romantic's wishing for release from the shackles of life (Shelly's "O lift me as a leaf, a wave, a cloud, / I fall upon the thorns of life, I bleed";) for example – is indicative of that quality in aspiration, in praying for Grace, in hope or despair, in pleading, and in any kindred nuances which we experience following the awareness of some lack. It can be personal; it can be on behalf of another (when we practise intercession); it can express concern of a wider situation – it can be as altruistic as possible. In wishing, the soul truly reaches out, but there is no guarantee of 'arrival'.

The above points towards the soul's inner movements in wish, wonder and surprise. Having found a way to make the class aware of each quality, the pedagogical task is to assist the finding of the way become a permanently enriching life experience for the being-born astral body of the youth. As a warm-up in the rhythmic part of the

Notes

lesson, we can practise speaking small phrases in chorus in a dramatic tone of voice:

{"If *only* I had heeded her advice!"}
{"Did you *ever* see anything like it?"}
{"We've *made* it..."}.

These, and a multitude of similar vernacular-like exercises having been 'declaimed', and if the class has enjoyed the melodramatic potential of the exercise, the task might be given of writing a short story leading up to each declamation. Whatever they felt in the brief moment of voicing the phrases in wishful, wondrous or surprise fashion, can then grow into the full point at which it becomes, so to speak, the ripened seed.

Conversely, a written task can be initiated at the other end, the teacher giving the opening phrase which then has to be continued. It is ideal if the situation depicted in the given opening is self-explanatory as regards mood, so that the children's intellect does not need to be stimulated abstractly with some such instruction as: 'Continue the following, expressing the quality of surprise.' The dry intellect and what is being engendered here are not necessarily mutually supportive; indeed, the former can impede the latter. This does not constitute a setback overall: intellect is cultivated elsewhere. Thus the pump can be primed with something like:

{It had been a long day with a hectic backlog of work in the office. "Let's take a walk on the beach," said the two colleagues as they stepped into the

street and gulped a lungful of salty sea air, "there's still a good hour of winter sun left." The beach was deserted. They strolled to the far end of the bay as the tide was out, though the breakers could still be heard exulting in the caves carved out of the precipitous cliff face. Jacquie, their little terrier, suddenly started barking excitedly. As they turned round a rocky corner, to their dismay, jutting out of the sea-wrack-carpeted sand, they saw...}

or

{Almost dropping with fatigue, yet elated with the bracing mountain air, they reached the summit. Never before had a sunrise seemed...}

or

{Shaken, she put down the phone. That gang again! Abandoning her son in the old warehouse! Fallen and couldn't move his leg! She scraped a few essentials into her handbag, dashed down stairs out onto the traffic-snarled street and in desperation...}

first being dictated.

The other main-lessons of the year offer ample opportunity to put what has been set in motion into practice. Of course, the wealth of material – astronomy, human biology, Renaissance and Reformation history, the discoveries etc. – will make much wider written English demands. But from time to time the teacher will be able to cash in on certain situations, particularly perhaps when initiating the world geography

Notes

Notes

main-lesson with what Steiner refers to as the 'spiritual geography' of the country concerned:

{At the top of the gigantic-stepped pyramids, the Aztecs placed their victims on the blood-stained altar...}
{The white men were amazed to see the ritualistic marks on the Aboriginals' skins...}
{The young heroes were led by the tribes' elders into the savannah for their initiation...}.

Even more specific moments in history will call for vivid descriptions:

{His crew's terror having reached boiling point, Columbus...}
{As the flames began to encircle the Maid, tied to the stake and with her eyes lifted to heaven, one of the soldiers standing by...}
{Brunelleschi's moment had come: flinging the bandages off as he leapt out of bed, he ranted: "...}
{The poor beggar couldn't believe his luck. Leonardo placed a dish of...}
{News of the Portuguese fleet sailing south instead of north to Holland spread like wild fire, but it was too late for the Quetans to boost their defences. They...}.

So much for how the *what* can be projected into the work of the whole year – indeed, beyond the year into Class 8 etc. But to return to the methodology of the English main-lesson itself. Time-consuming though it is, time and again it has proved time well spent if the children's first written efforts can be immediately collected in and quickly 'marked' by the teacher, followed by a highlight from *each and every* child's book read out in class appreciatively (if done anonymously this also has its benefits), and a few suggestions penned into the books – in place of spelling or punctuation corrections – made by the teacher, which aims to widen the child's appreciation of *style*. Parallel to this, creative writing exercises can be conducted by the teacher whereby, starting with a simple sentence:

Notes

{The snow clouds looked ominous.},

the children build the scene piece by piece: first an adjective added:

{The dark-charcoal snow clouds looked ominous.},

then a subsidiary clause added to set the scene:

{As the stage coach struggled up the already slushy hill, the dark etc.},

then a phrase tagged on at the end:

{As the stage coach struggled … looked ominous, alarming the passengers

and causing the coachman to curse violently and crack the whip ever sharper over the poor horses' flanks.}.

And so on, until the style has been forged sufficiently for the children's imagination and developing skill to take over and take off. During such exercises, a pause can be inserted into the writing after ten minutes or so in which children individually are asked to read out a sentence or two of their own choosing to the rest of the class, thereby adding to the creative momentum.

In such ways, but retained as it were within, and issuing from the child's aesthetic-feeling 'middle realm', sentences will result which, while well balanced, consist of complex grammatical structures, as a prelude to embarking in Classes 8 and 9 on the conscious *analysis* of such sentences, clause by clause, phrase by phrase. All the above – together of course with other exercises which the teacher's creativity will devise – provides psychological strength, richness, beauty and creative faculty for the pupil as he or she crosses the third birth-threshold of childhood, heralded by the awakening consciousness that accompanies the gradual but milestone-making emancipation of the astral organism.

Class 7

Notes

The Interjection

The human being is a citizen of two worlds: earth and heaven – or in more philosophical terms the physical and the spiritual. The spiritual, moreover is not merely that realm which is associated with the life after death and associated conditions. Insofar as the *concepts* we form – even about the most mundane of things like hearth rugs or bus tickets – are not in themselves physical, they may also be termed spiritual. The soul (the third component of this trinity) encompasses both worlds and, during waking life, is a hive of thinking, feeling and willing activity, figure-of-eighting in its interaction between its relationship with its responses towards the two worlds of its citizenship. It would be explosively impossible to have all that is taking place in that hive in one's consciousness. We are highly selective, even when not particularly focused. At the same time, the hive of hive-buzzing inner activity does not cease. Indeed, it requires an unusually determined effort to empty the consciousness if, for instance, we wish it to become a chalice for receiving something that otherwise might not get a look in as far as our inner life is concerned.

The soul's lemniscatory activity is constantly pressing through into one's awareness, of its own accord, so to speak. When this happens in a way that is significant, very often the first sign that it *is* happening is only indistinctly registered – not something that we could put into words as crystal clear and formed as cut glass. Nevertheless, what is pressing through into our awareness, we express in primitive forms as *interjection.* Primitive in the sense of primary. Indeed the *primary interjections*, so called:

{ah, ooh, oh, ah, eh, mmm}

for instance – are malleable enough for the soul to convey their meaning, albeit indistinctly, through musically inflecting the voice. Taking them in turn as thinking, feeling, willing reactions, the following common-all-garden situations may serve to illustrate the point.

1a **"You simply *must* agree." "Mmmm, I'm not so sure."**
1b **"What do you think of it?" "Mmm: delicious."**
1c **"How about if we meet for coffee next Friday?" "Mm, sounds good!"**
2a **"So that's where I'm planning to go." "Ah: but haven't you overlooked..."**
2b **"They were born last night." "Ahh: they're so sweet."**
2c **"You can't catch me!" "Ahah, that's what you think!"**
3a **"I'm going to sit him in front of that broccoli until he eats it." "Ooh, isn't that going a step too far?"**
3b **"Ooh, that's my shin!"**

3c “And this is the cellar.” “Ooh: I’m not going down there.”

4a “And this is what they sent instead.” “Oh no! What will you do?”

4b “His leave has been cancelled.” “Oh ... I’ve just been online booking our hotel.”

4c “The post office is still on strike.” “Oh: I could scream.”

5a “There’s one in next door’s garden.” “Eh, you can’t just walk off with it.”

5b “And then I got this cheque in the post.” “Eh? Really?”

5c “It looks as though there’ll be a storm.” “Come on! Let’s just go, eh?”

The above could be multiplied ad infinitum by going into different grades and shades of thinking, feeling and willing, for which classroom practice will offer plenty of opportunities. As often as not, the interjection will spill over into words that initially have other meanings:

{“Oh heavens!” “Ah, holy smoke!” “Ooh, good grief!”
“Aha, then the cat’s out of the bag.” “Bah! I guessed it would be a write off.”
“Mm: there are two sides to every story.”}.

Or the *secondary interjection* may suffice on its own:

{“Dear me. I never would have suspected it.”}
{“Hello! I’m sure I left my case here.”}
{“Sadly, no!”}.

Notes

There are interjections which match fairly precise situations:

{"Brr – it's cold"}
{"Alas!"}
{"Ouch. That's my foot."}
{"Well I never."}
{"Yuck"}
{"Yummy!"}
{"Welladay!"}
{"Incredible!"}.

Not infrequently, the interjection will incorporate a certain consonantal sound which conveys the point at which the soul finds its breakthrough. The iron hardness of D comes out in:

{drat, darn it, damnation, the Devil}.

The bursting through quality of the hard G launches the 'gob-smacked' element that lives and lurks in interjections such as:

{gosh, good grief, golly, gadzooks, goodness gracious}.

The throw away, wash-my-hands-of-it element in R come across in:

{rubbish, rot, rats, rank idleness}.

(On a personal note, I knew a university librarian whose inner poise and normally undentable phlegma would gently wrap the R of her professional disapproval – if a volume had not been returned or renewed, for instance – in "[Name of miscreant borrower, said with lip-pursed melodrama, particularly if it was a senior academic member of staff], may whose RRRabbits die!" There are two sides (celebratory and frustrating) to B:

{bingo, biffing, bravo, blast, bone idle, botheration, blow (and other expletives)}.

Perhaps the power of the B to give vent to the soul's irascibility qualifies the sound to become regent of this particular interjectory realm. There was the case of the family who moved from Manchester to Berlin. The son struggled at school to acquire the second language. In spite of progress, on one occasion a situation occurred which brought his frustration to bursting point. He lanced the boil that had built up in his soul by hammering the table with clenched fist and uttering "B-L-eistift!" The situation was further calmed when – the ribald laughter having died away – his new friends sympathetically explained that the word was not an orthodox German curse, but that it simply meant *lead pencil*. Perhaps the "B-L" would have said it all on its own.

It has been some time now that the fashionable adolescent interjection has been 'cool'. 'Hello?' said with a tone that expressed irony was in favour for some years.

Notes

Ancestors of 'cool' going back to the 40s and 50s were:

{smashing, super, terrific, super-duper, champion, good show, whizzo, splendiferous},

all of them now usurped, at least in the media's interviewing by {absolutely}. During the Second World War, school boys latched on to 'spiff', a shortened form of 'spiffing' a shortened form of 'spifflicating'!! Or there was the somewhat sarcastic image of the girls' public school whose sports mistress would gain popularity with interjections like:

{'jolly hockey sticks'}

and so on. Interjections that occasionally come back in cycles rather than just fading out, or pop up as smacking something between archaicisms and old friends are

{'ahem', 'phew', 'ooh la la', 'tut-tut', 'well what d'you know?' 'awesome', 'wow', 'pst', 'O lord', 'glory be'}.

But people would differ as to what category to put this or that interjection into. Not that a creature as flighty as the interjection will tolerate being pigeon-holed!

That aside, by far the lion's share of the above, are those interjections beloved of puberty where a huge chunk of the world's-your-oyster abandonment resides. Why might this be? We saw when looking into the main-lesson for Class 7 entitled *Wish,*

Wonder and Surprise how it opened up the early adolescent's awareness of the landscape of the human soul, with its heights and depths, its lengths and breadths, its aspirations and disappointments in all three astral regions (thinking, feeling and willing). Also apparent is the wisdom of giving a main-lesson in *Health, Hygiene and Nutrition* at a time a little before the unbalanced subjectivity that sets in in adolescence, and which it so frequently spawns. While there is still the authoritatively guided objectivity of the teacher, lifestyles which have a serious effect on health (healthy, unhealthy), hygiene (hygienic, unhygienic) and nutrition (nutritious, malnutritious) can be contemplated so that the early schooling of the astral can, like 'charity', begin at home.

Thus when the ever-more emancipated astral hive of activity begins to make itself felt, it can be met, acknowledged, made aware of itself, invited to gaze into its heights and depths, be helped to see its potential for good or evil reflected from people's behaviour in the world, and find sources of self-knowledge through the investigation of the world of interjections. The interjection acts as does a match struck near the surface of a terrain (such as that of Vesuvius) from which sulphurous vapours issue forth. It ignites the burning interest that the evermore personalised burgeoning astral forces have in humanity's inherent astrality, and by projection, directs non-judgementally the same interest inwards as it continues to "look into the soul".

There are three more facets that may be worth touching on here before the teacher is left to her own creative devices.

Notes

1. While avoiding the plethora of interjections which (blasphemoulsy?) are derived from spiritual worlds – e.g. *struth* (God's truth) or *zounds* (to cite an archaicism that is deemed to originate from 'His wounds'} – one should perhaps be prepared to enter into the phenomenon if the pupils raise it. Originally, such interjections must have sounded an echo of that world which plays into earthly affairs e.g.

{Almighty Heavens!} {My God!} {Allah be praised!} {By Jove!}.

2. The class could be given a class project to find out common interjections in other languages – by asking friends and relatives whose native tongue is not English. Some, of course, have filtered into English usage:

{***que linda, mamma mia, bien, hoots awa', begorrah, Donner und Blitzen, why aye, ach so, komisch***}

and so on. They can by savoured as much for their sound, as for the context in which the native speaker uses them.

3. As so often, methodologically it can drive a point home if the teacher gets her class to be inventive on their own. For example: pair off the class, and get each child to make up a word or an expression that could serve as an interjection – e.g. *stickleback soup!* – then hand it on to their partner who has to express what it means. (Stickleback soup = *Whatever next!*) Perhaps enthusiasm would be stirred for a mini-enactment to follow next.

Apart from the fun side of it – and the study of grammar always benefits from having fun and humour stirred into its simmering cauldron – such exercises can help the cynic in the adolescent ('These adults, look at them, leaving the world in an appalling mess for us to deal with.') keep an eye on himself so that when the astral is budding and blossoming in the third septennial phase, its own propensity for losing its way, kicking destructively over the traces, straying from the beaten track etc., will point to the need of self-control, discrimination, responsibility, balance of soul and other ethical attributes of the ever-evolving ego, still in its comparatively elementary, perhaps fragile, state of incarnation (despite the bravado, arrogance, ingratitude, bumptiousness and the inconsiderate rudeness that can display itself on the outer surface). *Cor blimey! The expectations of some teachers!*

Notes

Class 8

Sentence Diagrams alla Waldorf

Having travelled the highways and (some) byways of basic grammar in Classes 3-7, the parts of speech and the tenses and moods of verbs, and having opened the creative writing door that leads to the conscious use and development of *style* that we saw culminating in the seventh class main-lesson of Wish, Wonder and Surprise, the teaching of grammar now turns to those more complex constructions which involve the juxtaposition, balance, order and aesthetic length of *clauses*. This strengthening addition to the writer's tools is approached analytically in Class 9; here in Class 8 it is approached via *sentence diagrams*. The example on the front cover of the book, as far as the sentence's content is concerned is for the teacher's benefit, but as far as the diagram's visual implications are concerned it encapsulates the components and aims of this essentially new branch of grammar teaching.

The drawing of a sentence diagram is preceded by identifying the *finite verbs* in the sentence (a topic worked at through Classes 5-7). and thus establishing which words form the clause of which the finite verb is the kernel. In the sentence:

Notes

{One way in which the BBC celebrated Octavia Hill's centenary in 2012 was by visiting that part of Kent where she eventually settled down to live and where the National Trust, which was foreseen by her to be a forthcoming need of the nation, naturally has one of its principal roots.},

the five finite verbs, *celebrated, was, settled down, was foreseen, has,* are clothed with their subjects and other parts of speech – one was '*was by visiting that part of Kent*', or later, '*which was foreseen by her to be a forthcoming need of the nation*' etc. – so that they interrelate and form the sentence, a sentence which might well serve as the opening of a short article or essay on her invaluable work, and that of other reformers in the nineteenth century, in their noble efforts to stem the antisocial, anti-human tide that was a by-product of the capitalism that resulted inevitably from the Industrial Revolution.

The pupil's second task in making a sentence diagram is then, having identified the number and content of the sentence's clauses, to draw a diagram (consisting of straight and curved lines, joined together or otherwise obviously related) which gives expression to and echoes the clauses of the sentence: their number, their structural relation, their relative prominence and, if possible, their meaning.

Identifying the number of clauses in a sentence is straightforward:

{It took Wilberforce persistent effort to get his first Bill for the prohibition of slavery passed in parliament.},

Notes

unless perhaps a clause is interrupted:

{The women's prisons, which Elizabeth Fry was thoroughly determined to reform, defy description.}.

Their structural relationship can be straightforwardly linear:

{"Dr Livingstone, I presume," was Stanley's famous and oft-quoted remark, when they met in the African jungle.};

or it can be intertwined:

{Having anxiously gazed at the face of each body that lay on the battle field, Anita, who was already in an advanced stage of pregnancy, to her great relief, found Garibaldi mercifully still alive, and got him taken to a crude shelter where she nursed him back to full health, without which, his campaign and indeed his whole life's mission would have remained tragically unfulfilled.}.

Whether straightforward (as in the first example above) or challengingly complex (as in the second), however, this part of drawing the sentence diagram offers the astral body the twofold nourishment that is at the heart of its needs: freedom and responsibility. The number of lines has to be exact, and their relationship has to be arguably defensible; but these rational (left hemisphere) components are balanced by the (right hemisphere) creative freedom in the shape of the diagram.

Notes

Turning to the third part of the task, there are several components that the pupil has at his disposal for bringing something of the sentence's meaning visually into the diagram. The form, length and gesture of each clause-related line, their relative prominence in the overall shape, colours that can be used to enhance this and, last but not least, hints of realism that each individual line as well as the overall form might suggest.

{The ideals of Liberté, Egalité and Fraternité were one thing; the tragic way in which the French Revolution deteriorated into a blood bath was another.}

lends itself to a pictorial representation that suggests the guillotine, for instance, as do the diagrams representing such sentences as:

{It was his genius of manoeuvrability as much as anything else that brought Nelson the victory at the Battle of the Nile.}

and

{The remarkable outcome of Garibaldi's victory over the Austrian army of occupation was his supporting the crowning of Victor Emmanuel as King of Italy, which seemed to go against all of his republican ideals, for which he had risked his life time and time again in South America as well as throughout the campaign of the Risorgimento.},

Notes

this last sentence lending itself to the use of the 'tricolore' bands red, white and green, colours which still remain the symbol of Italian liberation and unity.

'Liberation and Unity' provide a helpful stepping stone to understanding the rationale behind this Class 8 topic, one of Steiner's most brilliant pedagogical ventures. On the one hand we have the purpose of teaching grammar, that purpose to which Waldorf accords equal (if not greater) importance than the acquisition of knowledge: the development of character and, in this case particularly, strength of individuality. On the other hand, the greater command of the mother tongue an individual acquires, the greater will be the potential to communicate with others – in whatever circumstances. Moreover, one doesn't have to travel very far into Steiner's spiritual scientific researches before meeting his perception of how language has its spiritual counterpart to its earthly manifestation: the Angeloi's connection with the individual, the Archangeloi's connection with the language of the 'folk', the Exusii's connection with the Logos itself and so on.

The position of the sentence diagram in Class 8 becomes clear against the above background. After the build up of grammar through Classes 3-7 (its parts of speech, the tenses and the moods of its verbs etc.) and after the linguistic exploration of the soul's landscape pursued in the Wish, Wonder and Surprise main-lesson in Class 7 (with the creative writing through the year which follows in the lesson's wake), there comes the bird's eye view of how complexity of thought is expressed in the construction of sentences. Each finite verb is like the seed in a raspberry which is fleshed out with nouns and other parts of speech, the sentence being formed of the cluster of clauses which result from this. The bird, however, is still in flight. Hovering above, so to speak, its 'eye' sees the principle features of the grammatical topography below. Then when the astral body becomes further emancipated (in Class 9 etc.) its inherent curiosity can descend from the bird's-eye-view heights, alight on the ground of clear, awakening consciousness and discern the fine detail, thereafter carrying its well-earned prey of ego-strength upwards into the heights of its future destiny.

Notes

By the same author

1981 *Music for the Oberufer Christmas Plays, 1st Edition*

1982 *Weft for the Rainbow* (Poems for classroom recitation)

1987 *The Waldorf Song Book*

1989 Meteor Showers and Us (Poems for classroom recitation)

1990 *A Round of Rounds* (52 canons and rounds with English and German words)

1991 *Becoming a Steiner School*

1992 *Patter Paws the Fox* (A class reader)

1993 *The Second Waldorf Song Book*

1993 *Waldorf Curriculum Studies: Science* (Ed.)

1995 *Concordance: Rudolf Steiner / Waldorf Education*

1997 *An Appraisal of Steinerian Theory and Waldorf Praxis: How do they compare?*

1998 *Trumpets of Happiness* (A class reader)

1998 *Owen Barfield: A Waldorf Tribute* (Ed.)

2000 *Index: Child and Man / Steiner Education 1977-2000*

2005 *Adventures in Steiner Education*

2006 *Mozart: His musical style and his role in the development of human consciousness*

2007 *Steiner Education and Social Issues*

2009 *Keynotes in Life and Work: Perspectives gained from a life working with Steiner Education*

2010 *"Till thou comest there" : Leading Thoughts and Music for the Shepherds' Play from Oberufer*

2011 *con.gusto @ Three Score Years and Twenty*

2012 *Kindling the Word: The Karmic Background of Marie Steiner-von Sivers* (Co-Author)

2013 *Word-Song at Dawn: Verses for Recitation in Spring*

2013 *Words and Whey at Milking: Verses for Recitation in Summer*

2014 *Words of a Feather: Verses for Recitation in Autumn*

2016 *Word-Prints in the Snow: Verses for Recitation in Winter*